Paul Cookson and David Harmer are *Spill the Beans*.

Paul was born in 1961 in Essex but luckily he was brought up in Lancashire.

David was born in 1952 and very quickly moved from South London to Yorkshire.

After the usual exams and college courses both became teachers, but not at the same school or at the same time. Paul still teaches but spends most of his time working as a writer and performer. David is now a headteacher but spends much of his time writing and performing as well.

Paul and David are married, but not to each other. Paul lives with Sally, Sam and Daisy (and Ginger the guinea pig) in Retford and David lives with Paula, Lizzie, Harriet (and hordes of cats) in Doncaster.

Also availble from Macmillan

How to Embarrass Teachers
Poems Chosen by Paul Cookson

Give Us a Goal!
Football poems by Paul Cookson

Pants on Fire
Poems by Paul Cookson

Pirate Poems
By David Harmer

The Truth About Teachers
Hilarious rhymes by Paul Cookson, David Harmer,
Brian Moses and Roger Stevens

SPILL THE BEANS

Poems by

Paul Cookson

and

David Harmer

Illustrated by David Parkins

MACMILLAN CHILDREN'S BOOKS

Dedicated to our long-suffering families,
who regularly let us go out to play

First published 2000 by Macmillan Children's Books
a division of Macmillan Publishers Ltd
20 New Wharf Road, London N1 9RR
Basingstoke and Oxford
Associated companies throughout the world
www.panmacmillan.com

ISBN 978-0-330-39214-3

9 8

A CIP catalogue record for this book is available from the British Library.

Printed and bound in the UK by CPI Mackays, Chatham ME5 8TD

Contents

Introduction

SPILL THE BEANS were born on the 4th of February 1992 at St Bede's RC Primary School, Widnes. Since then, Paul and David have performed hundreds of shows in hundreds of different venues throughout the country. They are both prolific writers and editors whose poems can be found in a wide variety of collections and anthologies. They have written and appeared in Children's BBC TV programme, *Wham Bam Strawberry Jam* and between them have sold enough books to earn at least one gold disc. Paul spends most of his time giving performances and workshops in schools and libraries. David spends most of his time being a primary school headteacher.

This book brings together favourites old and new from their highly original, rock and roll poetry show. These poems need to be performed out loud on your own, with a friend, with lots of friends, in assemblies, in your classroom, on buses, behind the bike sheds and always loudly.

Paul and David are too old to be pop stars, but this is their live album.

Spill The Beans

Ess pee eye double ell
Ess pee eye double ell

Spill The Beans, Spill The Beans
That's who we are, we're Spill The Beans
Spill The Beans, Spill The Beans
That's who we are, we're Spill The Beans

Waddaweedoo——Spill The Beans
Waddaweedoo——Spill The Beans
What do we do, we spill those beans.

Ess pee eye double ell
Ess pee eye double ell
Ess pee eye double ell

Poems stories laughter jokes
All join in, so come on folks

Spill The Beans, Spill The Beans
That's who we are, we're Spill The Beans
Spill The Beans, Spill The Beans
That's who we are, we're Spill The Beans

Waddaweedoo——Spill The Beans
Waddaweedoo——Spill The Beans
Waddaweedoo——Spill The Beans
What do we do, we spill those beans!

Born In Widnes

Gigging in Wigan I get my kicks
Going up North on Route M6
Born in Widnes – mad March morning
Spill The Beans – not dead not boring!
Spill The Beans – not dead not boring!

Retford Sprotbrough Widnes Wigan
These are the places the Beans are big in
Rocking in Runcorn Rolling in Rotherham
Raving in Rochdale we're all over 'em.

Barnsley, Derby and Doncaster
No one does their poems faster
Born in Widnes – they weren't yawning
Spill The Beans – not dead not boring!
Spill The Beans – not dead not boring!

Retford Sprotbrough Widnes Wigan
These are the places the Beans are big in
Rocking in Runcorn Rolling in Rotherham
Raving in Rochdale we're all over 'em

Have Spill The Beans played the NEC?
    No, have we heck!
Have Spill The Beans played Wembley Stadium?
    No, have we heck!
Have Spill The Beans played the Sheffield Arena?
    No, have we heck!
Have Spill The Beans played the Barnsley Arena?
    We might if they build one.

Have Spill The Beans played the Lipton Village Festival in a
Small tin hut on Bodmin moor on a very quiet Easter
Sunday?

Yes we have!

Have Spill The Beans been banned from a school in
Birmingham for saying 'bum' in front of infants?

Yes we have!

Have Spill The Beans played at Morpeth
Library to a small boy in a Batman suit which
He didn't take off not even to laugh which
He didn't do much?

Yes we have! Yes we have!
These strange exotic places
With strange exotic faces
Paul and David's Antics Roadshow
There's no place that we should not go
Gigs are big gigs are small
Spill The Beans have played them all.

Retford Sprotbrough Widnes Wigan
These are the places
That the Beans are big in
Rocking in Runcorn Rolling in Rotherham
Raving in Rochdale we're all over 'em

A heaving hall couldn't fit any more in
If poems were goals we'd be scoring
No one sleeping no one snoring.
Spill The Beans – not dead not boring!
Spill The Beans – not dead not boring!

Parents cheering children roaring
Temperatures and pulses soaring
On the road and always touring
Spill The Beans – not dead not boring!
Spill The Beans – not dead not boring!

The two in Wigan were adoring
Spill The Beans – not dead not boring!

Riboflavin

SNAP CRACKLE POP POP POP
SNAP CRACKLE POP POP POP

Every morning in your bowl
A flake of sunshine to fill your soul
Every chunk you have to chew
Looks and tastes like used-up glue
Clogging the insides of you
With red and green revolting goo
I don't want to get polemical
But all of it is one big chemical

THIAMIN NIACIN VITAMIN VYTAMIN
THIAMIN NIACIN VITAMIN VYTAMIN
HAVE A BRAIN LIGHT AGAIN
HAVE AN EYE BRIGHT AGAIN
GRAB ANOTHER BITE OF
RIBOFLAVIN . . . LOTSA GOLDEN CORN
RIBOFLAVIN . . . LOTSA GOLDEN CORN
RIBOFLAVIN . . . LOTSA GOLDEN CORN

SNAP CRACKLE POP POP POP
SNAP CRACKLE POP POP POP

They do such things with corn
A flipping great cockerel on your lawn
A whole gang of kids you've never seen
All by appointment to the Queen
Bet she keeps her insides clean
With all that iron and protein
Watching companies getting wealthier
When eating the cardboard would be healthier

THIAMIN NIACIN VITAMIN VYTAMIN
THIAMIN NIACIN VITAMIN VYTAMIN
HAVE A BRAIN LIGHT AGAIN
HAVE AN EYE BRIGHT AGAIN
GRAB ANOTHER BITE OF
RIBOFLAVIN . . . LOTSA GOLDEN CORN
RIBOFLAVIN . . . LOTSA GOLDEN CORN
RIBOFLAVIN . . . LOTSA GOLDEN CORN

Mum Used Prittstick

Mum used Prittstick
Instead of lipstick
Then went and kissed my dad.

Two days passed
Both stuck fast
The longest snog they ever had.

Picnic Time On The M25

A true story! What a daft place for a picnic! P.S. the M69 is much nicer. By the way, it's fun to repeat each line when performing the verses.

Picnic time go for a ride
set your sights on the countryside
pack the car and start to drive
stop by the side stop by the side
stop by the side of the M25

Deck chairs on the grass verge
Watch the traffic pass NEEOWN!
Try and pour your flask
Ooh ah ooh ooh eeh
Boiling coffee on your knee

Picnic time go for a ride
set your sights on the countryside
pack the car and start to drive
stop by the side stop by the side
stop by the side of the M25

Salmon spread wholemeal bread
Try to eat as you move your head
Left to right try to bite
Ooh ah ooh ooh eeh
Salmon Spread on your knee

Picnic time go for a ride
set your sights on the countryside
pack the car and start to drive
stop by the side stop by the side
stop by the side of the M25

Picnic time on the M25
Toxic gases will collide
Car-bon di-oxide
Breathe in SNIFF!
Breathe in SNIFF!
Petrol fumes and lead oxide
Cough splutter cough choke
Poisoned lungs are no joke
Ooh ah ooh ooh eeh
Plan your picnics carefully
Seaside or countryside
But don't go down to the M25
Don't go down to the M25
Don't - pic - nic - on - the - M - Twenty-Five!

The Dinosaurs That Time Forgot

The dinosaur whose feet hurt
. . . the Pawsaresorus

The singing dinosaur
. . . the Repeatachorus

The dinosaur who likes to be noticed
. . . the Don'tignorus

The dinosaur with a head like a mop
. . . the Wipethefloorus

The loyal dinosaur
. . . The Alwaysforus

The criminal dinosaur
. . . the Lawlessaurus

The one that lights up the sky
. . . the Auroaborealisaurus

The dinosaur that's just been to the dentist
. . . the Jawsaresorus

The dinosaur who lies in damp caves
. . . the Wallsareporus

The footballing dinosaur
. . . the Alwaysscorus

The DIY dinosaur
. . . the Hammernailandcopingsawus

The dinosaur that likes puzzles
. . . the Morejigsawus

The dinosaur found in a bedroom
. . . the Chestofdrawerus

The dinosaur built from coloured plastic bricks
. . . the Legosaurus

The toyshop dinosaur
. . . the ToysRusastaurus

There's A Monster In The Garden

Be very, very scared . . . when you shout out 'Look everybody there's a monster in the garden! Yikes!' Be sure to raise your hands in a cartoon-like manner every time you shout 'Yikes!'

If the water in your fishpond fizzes and foams
And there's giant teeth marks on the plastic gnomes
You've found huge claw prints in the flower bed
And just caught sight of a two-horned head
Put a stick in your front lawn with a piece of card on
Look out everybody – there's a monster in the garden!
   Yikes!

You haven't seen the dustman for several weeks
Haven't seen the gasman who was looking for leaks
Haven't seen the paper-girl, postman or plumber
Haven't seen the window cleaner since last summer
Don't mean to be nosy, I do beg your pardon
Look out everybody – there's a monster in the garden!
   Yikes!

Monster monster ooo there's a monster!
Yikes Yikes
Get you get you, it's going to get you!
Yikes Yikes
Scare you scare you, it's going to scare you!
Yikes Yikes
Eat you eat you, it's going to eat you!
Yikes Yikes
Snog you, snog you, urgh it'll snog you!
Yikes, Yikes

One dark night it will move in downstairs
Start living in the kitchen, take you unawares
Frighten you, bite on you, with howls and roars
It will crash about, smash about, push you out of doors
In the cold and snow the ice and rain will harden
Look out everybody – there's a monster in the garden!
   Yikes!

Now listen to me neighbour, all of this is true
It happened next door now it's happening to you.
There's something nasty on the compost heat
Spends all day there curled up asleep
You don't want your bones crunched or jarred on
Look out everybody – there's a monster in the garden!
   Yikes!

If Your Pet Snake Escapes . . .

Don't kick the draught excluder behind the door.
It might bite back.

Don't help Great Auntie Alice with her feather boa
if you hear a hissing sound.
It could be a cunning disguise.

You may find that the hosepipe beside the watering can
does not fit easily onto the tap.

Check the waistband of your trousers carefully
and make sure that you find at least one buckle.

Do not try and pump up the tyre on your new mountain bike.
The sound you hear may not be a puncture.

The light cord in the bathroom may give you a nasty shock.
And it may not be electric.

Make sure that the tie backs don't start eating the curtains.

Tell your sister to be careful with her new clarinet,
especially which end she blows.

If the toilet seat is patterned . . . beware!

When you hear the sound of the baby's rattle
underneath your bed at night
be very very very very careful.
Especially if you haven't got a baby.

Let's Go Steelers, Let's Go

*Play your own Premier League Ice Hockey match with the mighty
Sheffield Steelers and their superhero captain Rocket Ron. All you
have to do is repeat the chorus and shout 'Steelers OO OO!' while
jabbing the air and not the person in front. Make sure you try to
sound like ten and a half thousand ice hockey fans. By the way,
see if you can spot the real ice hockey team name in the middle.*

LET'S GO STEELERS LET'S GO
LET'S GO STEELERS LET'S GO

Rocket Ron hits the ice
He cuts up rough, none too nice

At number ten trouble's brewing
Storming Steve leaves them a ruin

Slams that stick, a power play
Blows the other team away

LET'S GO STEELERS LET'S GO

Down the rink, in the groove
You should see these Steelers move

Sharp as lightning, fierce as thunder
Watch that other team go under

Ten more goals hit the slot
The ice is cold but the Steelers are hot

LET'S GO STEELERS LET'S GO

ROCKET RON!
STEELERS OO OO
ROCKET RON!
STEELERS OO OO
ROCKET RON!
STEELERS OO OO

LET'S GO STEELERS LET'S GO

We defeat so many teams
Freezing up their hopes and dreams

Give them all such a belting
Move so fast the ice is melting

Start off tall, but they end up sore
None of these came back for more

The Retford Rotters and the Sprotbrough Slugs
The Wigan Winkles and the Bedford Bugs
The Barnsley Bottoms and the Scarborough Slackers
The Luton Loafers and the Crewe Cream Crackers
The Dudley Duds and the Salisbury Sillies
The Nuneaton Nutters and the Wellington Willies
The Greasborough Greasers and the Shrewsbury Shrews
They all get the losing-to-the-mighty-Steelers blues

LET'S GO STEELERS LET'S GO

The Amazing Captain Concorde

A do it yourself superhero poem complete with actions and sound effects . . .

IS IT A BIRD? (Raise your right hand above your eyes and look right)

IS IT A PLANE? (Raise your left hand above your eyes and look left)

LOOK AT THE SIZE OF THE NOSE ON HIS FACE! (point to your nose)

IS IT A BIRD? (Repeat as above)

IS IT A PLANE? (Repeat as above)

CAPTAIN CONCORDE IS HIS NAME! (Salute with right hand)

CAPTAIN CONCORDE NEEEEOOWN! (Salute then stretch out both arms)

CAPTAIN CONCORDE NEEEEOOWN! (Salute then stretch)

IS IT A BIRD?
IS IT A PLANE?
LOOK AT THE SIZE OF THE NOSE ON HIS FACE!
IS IT A BIRD?
IS IT A PLANE?
CAPTAIN CONCORDE IS HIS NAME!
CAPTAIN CONCORDE NEEEEOOWN!
CAPTAIN CONCORDE NEEEEOOWN!

A man with a mission
Radar vision
A nose that's supersonic
Faster than the speed of sound
His Y-fronts are bionic
Big and baggy
Red and saggy
Streamlined underpants
Always ready
Hi-tech sheddies
Crooks don't stand a chance

IS IT A BIRD?
IS IT A PLANE?
LOOK AT THE SIZE OF THE NOSE ON HIS FACE!
IS IT A BIRD?
IS IT A PLANE?
CAPTAIN CONCORDE IS HIS NAME!
CAPTAIN CONCORDE NEEEEOOWN!
CAPTAIN CONCORDE NEEEEOOWN!

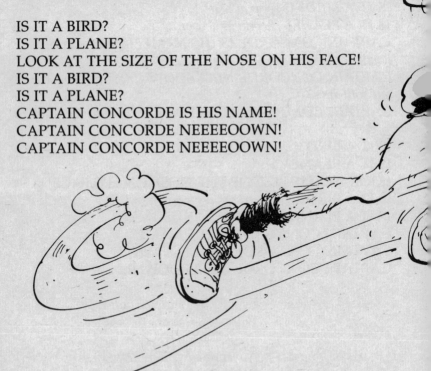

Anytime anyplace anywhere
But never ever Mondays
Coz that's the day the Captain's mum
Washes his red undies

Anytime anyplace anywhere
His power is fantastic
Everything's under control
With super strength elastic

Anytime anyplace anywhere
But bathrooms are a no no
Coz the toilet seat has teeth – Ow!
And then it's time to go so . . .

IS IT A BIRD?
IS IT A PLANE?
LOOK AT THE SIZE OF THE NOSE ON HIS FACE!
IS IT A BIRD?
IS IT A PLANE?
CAPTAIN CONCORDE IS HIS NAME!
CAPTAIN CONCORDE NEEEEOOWN!
CAPTAIN CONCORDE NEEEEOOWN!

The Amazing Captain Concorde . . . he's a superman
The Amazing Captain Concorde . . . super underpants
The Amazing Captain Concorde . . . nobody can trick him
The Amazing Captain Concorde . . . with a nose like that
   you'd pick him.

Who's the man with the supersonic nose? . . .
   Captain Concorde!
Who's the man with horrible taste in clothes? . . .
   Captain Concorde!
Who's the man who's always your best friend? . . .
   Captain Concorde!
Who's the man who's always set the trend? . . .
   Captain Concorde!
Who's the man who's so aerodynamic? . . .
   Captain Concorde!
Who's the man who makes the villains panic? . . .
   Captain Concorde!
Who's the man who always helps his mum? . . .
   Captain Concorde!
Who's the man you'd like to become? . . .
   Captain Concorde!
Who? Captain Concorde!
Who? Captain Concorde!
So . . .

IS IT A BIRD?
IS IT A PLANE?
LOOK AT THE SIZE OF THE NOSE ON HIS FACE!
IS IT A BIRD?
IS IT A PLANE?
CAPTAIN CONCORDE IS HIS NAME!
CAPTAIN CONCORDE NEEEEOOWN!
CAPTAIN CONCORDE NEEEEOOWN!

Stuck Behind The Man With The Caravan

This poem is about David's hobby. Paul hates it – guess who's who.

He's stuck
Stuck behind the man
He's stuck
Stuck behind the man
He's stuck
Stuck behind the man
Stuck behind the man with the caravan
Stuck behind the man with the caravan
That's me   *... that's him ...*

I'm the man with the caravan
  And I'm the man behind
I've got all the weekend
  And I haven't got the time

Bank Holiday country road
Caravan with a heavy load
In my mirror I can see
Twenty-five cars trying to pass me ...

I'm two hours late already
I just can't drive this steady
Gotta put my foot down gotta get past
Gotta get there gotta get there fast!
Gotta get there gotta get there fast!

He's stuck
Stuck behind the man
He's stuck
Stuck behind the man
He's stuck
Stuck behind the man
Stuck behind the man with the caravan
Stuck behind the man with the caravan
That's me   . . . *that's him* . . .

   Is that a gap in front (gasp!)?
   Is that a gap in front (gasp!)?
I'm going to the middle
I'm going to the middle
I'm going to the middle little by little
   I'm trying to overtake it
   I'm trying to overtake it
   I'm trying to overtake it
   I'm never going to make it . . .

You're stuck . . . hard luck!
You're stuck . . . hard luck!

He's stuck
Stuck behind the man
He's stuck
Stuck behind the man
He's stuck
Stuck behind the man
Stuck behind the man with the caravan
Stuck behind the man with the caravan
That's me   . . . *that's him* . . .

A big white "P" in front of me
There's a lay-by up ahead
I could make them smile
pull over for a while
but I think I'll
slowly drive five more miles
in style in style instead!

Oh! No! Drat! Blast!
Look at that! He's gone right past!
Goodbye lay-by I've gotta drive by
I'm gonna cry if I don't get by
Stuck here till I'm past my sell-by date,
I'm late, trying to accelerate
this state is great, this bloke is gonna make me wait,
* aggravate, frustrate, agitate, make me hate!*

He's stuck
Stuck behind the man
He's stuck
Stuck behind the man
He's stuck
Stuck behind the man
Stuck behind the man with the caravan
Stuck behind the man with the caravan
That's me . . . *that's him* . . .

Sooner or later sooner or later
he's got to use his indicator
Left or right I don't care
He could go anywhere
Look there! Look there!
He's turning off just there!
Yippee! I'm free!
Open road in front of me
I'll just get round this bend . . .
Oh no! Not again!

Tough luck, I'm back
I found a short cut down this track
You're stuck, you're stuck
just like you were before
   And I can't stand it any more!

He's stuck
Stuck behind the man
He's stuck
Stuck behind the man
He's stuck
Stuck behind the man
Stuck behind the man with the caravan
Stuck behind the man with the caravan
Stuck behind the man with the
brilliant   . . . *awful*
wonderful   . . . *terrible*
leisurely   . . . *slowcoach*
glorious   . . . *horrible*
up-to-date   . . . *snailpace*
white and shiny   . . . *driving me bonkers*
Stuck behind the man, stuck behind the man
Stuck behind the man with the caravan
That's me   . . . *That's him*

The Toilet Seat Has Teeth!

Be very, very scared . . . it's even worse than the monster in the garden and it bites you on the b . . . b . . . b . . . behind. Repeat 'the toilet seat has teeth! Oooh!' as many times as you want. For dramatic effect rise from your seat when you shout 'Oooh!'

The bathroom has gone crazy
far beyond belief.
The sink is full of spiders
and *the toilet seat has teeth! Ooh!*

The plughole in the bath
has a whirlpool underneath
that pulls you down feet first
and *the toilet seat has teeth! Ooh!*

The toothpaste tube is purple
and makes your teeth fall out.
The toilet roll is nettles
and makes you scream and shout!

The towels have got bristles,
the bubble bath is glue,
the soap has turned to jelly
and it makes your skin bright blue.

The hot tap gushes forth
with a sludge that is bright pink.
The cold tap dribbles lumps
of green that block the sink.

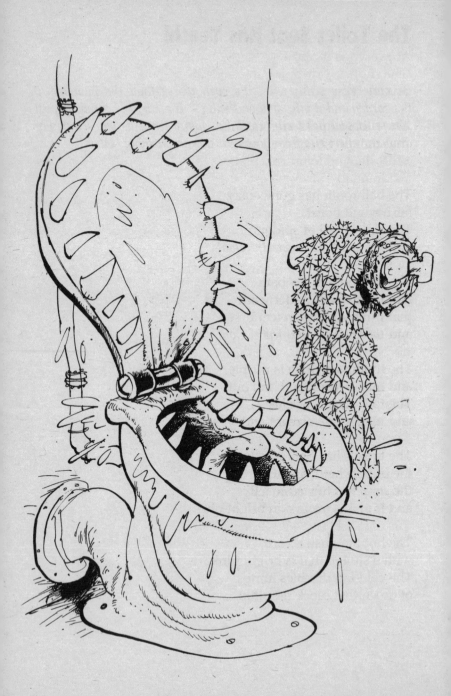

The mirror's pulling faces
at everyone it can.
The shower's dripping marmalade
and blackcurrant jam.

The rubber ducks are breeding
and building their own nest
with shaving foam and tissues
in Grandad's stringy vest.

Shampoo is liquid dynamite,
there's petrol in the hairspray,
both will cure dandruff
when they blow your head away!

The bathroom has gone crazy
far beyond belief.
The sink is full of spiders
and *the toilet seat has teeth! Ooh!*

The toilet seat has teeth! *Ooh!*
The toilet seat has teeth! *Ooh!*
The toilet seat has teeth! *Ooh!*
The toilet seat has teeth! *Ooh!*

Crunch! Slurp! Munch! Burp!
The toilet seat has teeth! Ooh!
Don't – sit – on – it!
The toilet seat has . . . ! Ohhhhhhhhhhhh!

The Tweaky Leaky Squeaky
Brand New School Shoe Blues

*New school shoes can tweak, squeak and sometimes leak. This is
what happens when they do all three. It's fun to do the sound
effects (more fun than wearing the shoes anyway).*

Mum has said I can't choose
the latest fashion front page news
so she bought me a pair of shoes
that are far too tight and I just can't use
I take size six but they feel like twos
cos they tweak my feet like tightened screws
they rub red raw, batter and bruise
pinks and purples, blacks and blues

Blister blister I've got a blister
Bigger than the bonce on my big sister

It's freaky when they're tweaky
and they're leaky and they're squeaky
Got a tweak in my shoes (Ooh!)
Got a leak in my shoes (Squelch!)
Got a squeak in my shoes (Eeh!)
Got a tweak and a leak and a squeak in my shoes
(Ooh! Squelch! Eeh!)
Got a tweak and a leak and a squeak in my shoes
(Ooh! Squelch! Eeh!)

Cold wet water starts to ooze
shoes like two new swimming pools
tidal waves like flushing loos

feet are paddling like canoes
toes that feel like damp cashews
soaking socks and woollen strews
insects swim and creatures cruise
through the oceans in my shoes

Blister blister I've got a blister
Bigger than the bonce on my big sister

My feet are bathed in bandages
My blister plaster stings.

There's so much water ankles ought to
wear some water wings

I just cannot go down town in
shoes that twist my toes around in
they tweak so much that I am frowning.
The water's such I am drowning.

New shoes, new shoe blues
I have got the new shoe blues

New shoes, new school shoes,
new school uncool new shoe blues.

I have got the blues
the brand new school shoe blues

Blister blister I've got a blister
Bigger than the bonce on my big sister

Big Bad Barry The Bully

Was tough.
Really tough.
The only seven-year-old Sumo wrestler at our school.

He was so tough he used to bully dinner ladies.

Only one at a time though.
Barry had tattoos.
Real ones, not like those you get out of penny bubblies
where you lick your arm and remove the paper . . .
Pirate ship, skull and crossbones.
No he had real ones, done with a needle.

Some were done with a needle and thread.
When he ran out of tattoos
His mum sewed anorak badges all over him
And he could tell exactly where he'd been for his holidays.

He'd been to Armthorpe
You could see that one on his arms
He'd been to Chester
You could see that one on his chest.
He'd been to Headingly
You could see that one on his head.
He'd been to Neasden.
You could see that one on his knees.
He'd been to Anklesea
You could see that one on his ankles.
He'd been to Ramsbottom
You could see that one behind the bikesheds
For three packets of bubbly and some wine gums.

And he'd been to Goole.
Twice.
Luckily they don't do a badge from there.

Mister Moore

Mister Moore, Mister Moore
Creaking down the corridor.

Uh uh eh eh uh
Uh uh eh eh uh

Mister Moore wears wooden suits
Mister Moore's got great big boots
Mister Moore's got hair like a brush
And Mister Moore don't like me much.

Mister Moore, Mister Moore
Creaking down the corridor.

Uh uh eh eh uh
Uh uh eh eh uh

When my teacher's there I haven't got a care
I can do my sums, I can do gerzinters
When Mister Moore comes through the door
Got a wooden head filled with splinters.

Mister Moore, Mister Moore
Creaking down the corridor.

Uh uh eh eh uh
Uh uh eh eh uh

Mister Moore I implore
My earholes ache, my head is sore
Don't come through that classroom door
Don't come through that classroom door.
Mister Mister Mister Moore
He's creaking down the corridor.

Uh uh eh eh uh
Uh uh eh eh uh

Big voice big hands
Big voice he's a very big man
Take my advice, be good be very very nice
Be good be very very nice
To Mister Moore, Mister Moore
Creaking down the corridor

Uh uh eh eh uh
Uh uh eh eh uh

Mister Moore wears wooden suits
Mister Moore's got great big boots
Mister Moore's got his hair like a brush
Mister Moore don't like me much

Mister Moore, Mister Moore
Creaking down the corridor.

Uh uh eh eh uh
Uh uh eh eh uh

I Want I Want I Want
(The Parents' Revenge Poem)

This is the parental revenge poem. We've noticed that kids don't say 'Please dear father may I have one of those items in the shop window as I do believe that my friend Rupert has one awfully similar . . .' No, they shout . . .

I want I want I want I want
Gimme that gimme that pleeaase!
I want I want I want I want
Gimme that gimme that pleeaase!

I want a doll I want a bike
And I want a football
I want a CD I want a Gameboy
I want that video.

Gimme a Mars Bar gimme some crisps
And I want some ice cream
Gimme a burger gimmee some chips
And a big thick milkshake

I want I want I want I want
Gimme that gimme that pleeaase!
I want I want I want I want
Gimme that gimme that pleeaase!

Dad Dad I want it now!
Mum Mum I want it now!
Da-ad pleeaase! *No way!*
Mu-um pleeaase! *No way!*

We're not made of money
It does not grow on trees
We're sick of all your mithering
And our demands are these

We want we want we want we want
Give us this give us this pleeaase!
We want we want we want we want
Give us this give us this pleeaase!

We want peace we want quiet
and we'd like a lie-in
We want rest we want sleep
We want your bedroom TIDY!

We're sick of all children's programmes
Those stupid children's programmes
And turn that Hi Fi down
Do you call that music?
That noisy modern racket
It's nothing like the Beatles! Yeah Man!

Modern telly?	. . .	*Rubbish!*
Cartoons?	. . .	*Rubbish!*
Morning telly?	. . .	*Rubbish!*
Computer games?	. . .	*Rubbish!*
Boy bands?	. . .	*Rubbish!*
Girl bands?	. . .	*Hang on a minute.*
		I quite like girl bands.

I want a doll	*We want peace*
I want a bike	*We want quiet*
I want a football	*We want a lie in*
I want a CD	*We want rest*
I want a Gameboy	*We want sleep*
I want a video	*Clean your bedroom*
I want a Mars bar	*Fold your clothes up*
I want crisps	*Do the dishes*
I want an ice cream	*Brush your teeth*
I want a burger	*Do your homework*
I want chips	*Tidy your school bag*
I want a milkshake	*Get out of my sight*
I want it now I want it now	*Out of my sight*
I want it now I want it now	*Out of my sight*
I want it now I want it now	*I've had him up to here*
I want it now I want it now	*All he ever says is*
I want it now I want it now.	*All he ever says is*

I want I want I want I want
Gimme that gimme that pleeaase!
I want I want I want I want
Gimme that gimme that pleeaase!

NO!!!!

My Dad The Headmaster

My dad the Headmaster knows every single rule
And when he is at home he thinks that he's at school.
He rings the bell each morning and I'd better not be late
so I'm washed and down for breakfast at exactly ten to eight.

He stands and takes the register, checks my shirt and tie,
then says "Good Morning" and I have to reply
"Good Morn - ing Fa - ther" in that monotone drone
and hear his assembly in my very own home.

He has a list of rules that are pasted on each door:
No Spitting. No Chewing. No Litter On The Floor.
No Music. No Jewellery. No Make-up. No Telly.
No Making Rude Noises Especially If They're Smelly.

No Videos. No Football. No Coloured Socks Or Laces
No Trainers. No Jeans. No Smiling Faces
No Sticking Bubble Gum In Your Sister's Hair
No Wiping Bogeys Down The Side Of The Chair.

He has a list of sayings for all types of occasion
and set of phrases for every situation:
"Don't run down the stairs. Speak when spoken to.
Put your hand up first if you want to use the loo."

"I don't mind how long I wait. Listen when I'm speaking.
No one leaves the table until we've finished eating.
Don't interrupt and don't answer back.
Don't do this and don't do that."

My dad the Headmaster knows every single rule
and when he is at home he thinks that he's at school.
But I'm not the only one who does what he is told.
Dad never complains if his dinner is cold.

He's ever so polite when Mother is around
and mumbles "Yes my dear" while looking at the ground.
Her foghorn commands, they really drive him crazy.
Dad's scared of Mum 'cause she's a dinner lady!

Deep, Dark, Strange And Nasty Secrets In The Staffroom

When Paul and David were at Junior School there was always one room you could never go in – this one. Now we know why . . .

There are deep, dark, strange and nasty
secrets in the staffroom
when the teachers escape at break
from the confines of the classroom.
What's behind, what do we find
behind the staffroom door?
What lurks inside, what secrets hide
Behind the staffroom door?

There are a thousand cups unfinished
all covered in green mould.
Coffee stains and rings remain
where they have overflowed.
Piles of files, unmarked books
and last term's lost reports,
the P.E. teacher's sweaty vest
and Lycra cycling shorts.

There are last week's lunch leftovers,
yoghurt pots and crusts,
banana skins and cola tins
all covered in chalk dust.
Examination papers
from nineteen sixty-eight
and the Times Ed job section
that's ten years out of date.

The ashtray's overflowed
and it's seeping out the door.
The wind has blown a million sheets
of paper on the floor.
There's paper planes and brown tea stains
from last night's staff meeting.
This place is a downright disgrace
not fit for a pig to eat in.

Inside the fridge half-finished milk
is lumpy and it's glowing.
The cartons are all starting
to mutate and they are growing.
The crockery mountain in the sink
is coated in green lime
and the room that time forgot
is left to rot in gunge and slime.

There are deep, dark, strange and nasty
secrets in the staffroom
when the teachers escape at break
from the confines of the classroom.
What's behind, what do we find
behind the staffroom door?
What lurks inside, what secrets hide
Behind the staffroom door?

Beware the creatures from this place,
the ones who always say
*"no one leaves the classroom
until this mess is cleared away!"*
But if you said the same to them
one thing is very clear
to get the staffroom spick and span
would take at least a year
   . . . or two . . . or three . . . or four . . . or maybe even more!

Mrs Terminator

The world's most frightening dinner lady. Shout out the chorus and pretend you're a dalek. PS. Mrs Terminator wasn't her real name. Her real name was Arthur.

Mrs Terminator – patrols the corridor
Mrs Terminator – paces up and down the floor
Mrs Terminator – her nostrils flare and steam
Breathing fire her face turns red when she begins to scream

Exterminate! Exterminate! Zap! Pow! Weeee!
Exterminate! Exterminate! Zap! Pow! Weeee!

Mrs Terminator – points and waves her hands
Mrs Terminator – bellows out her strict commands
Mrs Terminator – the veins upon her skull
Bulge and bubble just like pipes about to burst when full

Exterminate! Exterminate! Zap! Pow! Weeee!
Exterminate! Exterminate! Zap! Pow! Weeee!

Mrs Terminator – twenty-seven stone
Mrs Terminator – plays rugby on her own
Mrs Terminator – knuckles on the floor
Muscles just like Popeye's and whiskers on her jaw

Exterminate! Exterminate! Zap! Pow! Weeee!
Exterminate! Exterminate! Zap! Pow! Weeee!

Mrs Terminator – her favourite word is SILENCE!
Mrs Terminator – her favourite hobby's violence
Mrs Terminator – her school needs no bell
When she coughs the whole place stops and staff are scared
    as well

Exterminate! Exterminate! Zap! Pow! Weeee!
Exterminate! Exterminate! Zap! Pow! Weeee!

Frankenstein in a floral flock, Godzilla with the gravy
Dracula with a spatula . . . Monster dinner lady . . .
Razorblades for breakfast, cement and rocks for lunch
At tea she likes to hear the sound of children's bones go
    crunch
All washed down with petrol, acid, beer and meths
And everybody's trying to hide from her dragon breath

Exterminate! Exterminate! Zap! Pow! Weeee!
Exterminate! Exterminate! Zap! Pow! Weeee!

Mrs Terminator – sharp ears and X-ray vision
Mrs Terminator – no one questions her decision
Mrs Terminator – B.O. and halitosis
When she shouts she often spouts and drowns those who
    are closest

Exterminate! Exterminate! Zap! Pow! Weeee!
Exterminate! Exterminate! Zap! Pow! Weeee!

Mrs Terminator – checks that plates are clean
Mrs Terminator – makes you eat your greens
Mrs Terminator – she's a Sumo queen
Believes that staff and pupils should not be heard or seen

Exterminate! Exterminate! Zap! Pow! Weeee!
Exterminate! Exterminate! Zap! Pow! Weeee!

She's a Dalek dinner lady, drives the kids and teachers crazy
Mrs Terminator is the boss . . . RIGHT!
She'll be back to see you later, she is Mrs Terminator
Mrs Terminator is the big big big BIG BOSS!

Exterminate! Exterminate! Zap! Pow! Weeee!
Exterminate! Exterminate! Zap! Pow! Weeee!

Potty Pets

My dad's potty about pets
He breeds them
and he cross-breeds them.

He crossed a gorilla with a poodle.
Now we've got a Goroodle
Seven feet tall and very fierce
But it wears pink ribbons in its shaved fur.

Then he crossed a snake with a dog.
We've got a Snog.
Very friendly, but no one wants to kiss it.

After that he tried a cat and a parrot.
That was boring.
We got a Carrot.

Dad found the cross between the guinea pig and the hare
    very useful.
It lives on his bald head.
A Guinea Wig.

He crossed a squirrel and a worm.
Now he's got a long pink hairy squirm from the Wirral.

He crossed some ants with a pig.
Got some pants that grunt.

Then he tried crossing a mynah bird with a herd of
    bullocks . . .
and got a bird that talks a lot of baloney.

Mum made Dad stop though.
She didn't like it when he tried crossing
the elephant and the duck.
And believe me when the elephant flies over your head
. . . you have to
Duck!

FOUR FISHY TALES

Love Potion In The Sun Tan Lotion

In Spain on the beach for a tan
Miss Watson's adventure began

She slept as she swept out to sea
dreaming of us in Year Three.

Unseen a shark swam beneath
her airbed with razor sharp teeth.

It bit and she hit the water
just as a jellyfish caught her.

It stung, she awoke with a cry
saw no land, just blue sea and sky.

There was simply no one to save her
the shark could savour the flavour.

But then a small submarine
contrived to arrive on the scene.

She climbed in, the shark couldn't nip her
that summer she married the skipper.

Advice To A Heartbroken Shark

When Sharon the shark split up with him
Shaun didn't understand
But his best friends tried to cheer him up
'There's plenty more folk on the land!'

The Manta Pray

The manta ray began to pray
A fact most fish found odd
The manta ray began to pray
because he believed in . . . *Cod!*

Ocean Portions, Whale Size Proportions

Every night is fast food night
The whale thought licking his lips
Something slimy something crunchy
I know, fish and *ships*.

More Dinosaurs That Time Forgot

The beach-loving dinosaur
. . . the Sandyshorus

The uncertain dinosaur
. . . the NowI'mnotsosurus

The high-rise dinosaur
. . . the Multistoreysaurus

The home help dinosaur
. . . the Householdchorasurus

The short-sighted dinosaur
. . . the Tyrannosaurus Specs

The hooligan dinosaur
. . . the Tyrannosaurus Wrecks

The weightlifting dinosaur
. . . the Tyrannosaurus Pecs

The dinosaur who loves Chinese food
. . . the Friedriceatops and Sweetandsourporkasaurus

The law-enforcing dinosaur
. . . the Triceracops

The magical dinosaur
. . . the Diplohocuspokus

The blurred dinosaur
. . . the Diplo-outoffocus

The dinosaur that likes bonfires
. . . Diplochokasmokus

The flying dinosaur that's always late
. . . the Terrywon'tbebacktill

The drunken flying dinosaur
. . . the Verymerrydactyl

The farming dinosaur
. . . the Velocitractor

The dinosaur that's pulled a muscle
. . . the Velocirupture

Percy Is A Punk

We need some punk guitars here – get those air guitars out now for the 'Daggadaggadaggadagga' bits. We also need punk hairstyles. Use your hands as mohican hairstyles and nod when you shout 'Oy!' Shout it out, fast and loud! 1 - 2 - 3 - 4! Off you go!

1 2 3 4 Daggadaggadaggadagga! (x4)

Percy is a punk OY! (x4)

1 2 3 4 Daggadaggadaggadagga! (x4)

Percy is a punk OY! (x4)

Give us a   P! . . . P!
Give us an   E! . . . E!
Give us an   R! . . . R!
Give us a   C! . . . C!
Give us a   Y! . . . Y!
What does that spell? Percy!

1 2 3 4 Daggadaggadaggadagga! (x4)

Percy is a punk OY! (x4)

Percy is a
Percy is a
Percy is a . . . PUNK! OY!

Unzip Your Lips

Unzip your lips and get to grips
To the beat that skips so let it rip.
Rhyming rhythms for twisting tongues
Gonna rhyme those rhythms all day long.
Gonna roll those rhythms, rhyme those rocks
Gonna twist and tie your tongue in knots.

Goodness gracious! Great balls of fire!
Spill The Beans gonna take you higher!
A wop bop a loo bop a lop bam boom!
Spill The Beans gonna shake the room!
Be bop a lula she's my baby!
Spill The Beans gonna drive you crazy!
Twist and shout! Shake, rattle and roll!
OK Beanettes off you go . . .

DOO WOP WOP
BOP BOP SHOWADDYWADDY
A WOP BOP A LOO BOP A LOP BAM BOOM
BABY BABY BABY
WIGWAM BAM BAM SCAM A LAM
TUTTIFRUITI THAT'S ALL RIGHT MAMA
WEER ALL CRAZEE NOW! YEAH

Unzip your lips and shake your hips
Spill The Beans' greatest hits
Unroll your tongue, turn up the watts
Unlock the locks in your voice box
Gonna shake your tonsils, rattle your teeth
Roll vocal chords beyond belief

Gonna rock around the clock tonight!
Spill The Beans gonna set your soul alight!
Bless my soul what's wrong with me!
Spill The Beans gonna set you free!
Feel the noise and hit the groove!
Spill The Beans gonna raise the roof!
Twist and shout! Shake, rattle and roll!
OK Beanettes off you go . . .

DOO WOP WOP
BOP BOP SHOWADDYWADDY
A WOP BOP A LOO BOP A LOP BAM BOOM
BABY BABY BABY
WIGWAM BAM BAM SCAM A LAM
TUTTIFRUITI THAT'S ALL RIGHT MAMA
WEER ALL CRAZEE NOW! YEAH

The Absolutely Fluent Martian Love Poem

How to become an alien (if you are not an infant):
1. *Stretch both ears upwards while saying 'jugga jugga jugga jugga'.*
2. *Use both index fingers as aerials that shoot from your head as you say 'Zooom zooom'.*
3. *Pretend you're swimming breast stroke as you say 'Whooooo whooooo'.*

Now you are truly ready to beam down and speak . . .

Jugga jugga jugga jugga
Zooom zooom
Jugga jugga jugga jugga
Zooom zooom
Jugga jugga jugga jugga
Zooom zooom   m
Whooooooo, whooooooo.   o

                   o

Nyik nyik   o
Flo bblob blab blob. Wheeep!   o
Z z   z z   o
Z z z z   z
Srekcink, gons gons. Erk!

Jugga jugga jugga jugga
Zooom zooom
Jugga jugga jugga jugga
Zooom zooom
Jugga jugga jugga jugga
Zooom zooom
Whooooooo, whooooooo.

Aaaaaaaaaaaaaachooo!
Whangeywhangywheyoowheyoowhaaa.
Grint
Harg. Fwaarghle.

Jugga jugga jugga jugga
Zooom zooom
Jugga jugga jugga jugga
Zooom zooom
Jugga jugga jugga jugga
Zooom zooom
Whoooooo, whoooooo.

Klarp Hoooooo
Dwobble dwibble dwop dwop
Vvvvvvvvvvv stnap, pmurt, slibbo.
Thurb.

What the poem says:

Two teachers sat alone at night
Beside the fire that flickers
He was wearing his string vest
And she had frilly (Sorry, it loses something in
translation round about here).

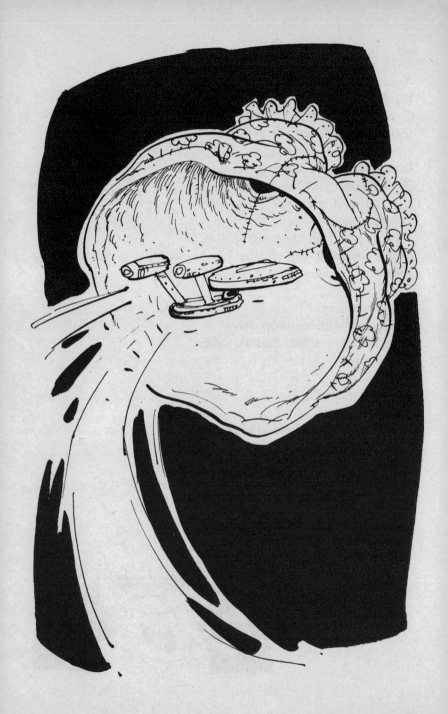

The Legend Of
Granny Grimble's Bloomers

There was once a granny called Grimble
Who spent most of her time out of doors
She lived in an old-fashioned village
And she wore the most old-fashioned drawers
The village was Trumpton-cum-Windy
A place most people pass through
Especially when she washed her bloomers
They're baggy, they're big and they're blue.

One day she was pegging her washing
Her smalls and her larges on t'line
To start with the weather was sunny
She thought she'd be done in fine time
But Trumpton-cum-Windy lived up to its name
A thunder storm started to brew
A gust of loose wind blew her gussets away
They're baggy, they're big and they're blue.

They flew off in th'air like a cyclone possessed
And hovered high over the church
Casting a shadow on what was below
Then swooped with a sickening lurch
At that very moment the village fête opened
With a speech from the Reverend Vickers
They fell on his head and swallowed him whole
Vicar Vickers was stuck in her knickers.

'What a to do,' Gran Grimble grumbled
'What a fuss, what a hullabaloo,
All because of some wind up my bloomers
They're baggy, they're big and they're blue.'

They extracted the vicar with hoots of delight
And excitable shouts from the crowd
'Ay up vicar, that's a grand marquee
By heck, tha's done us right proud.'
Working as one the job was soon done
The new tent was soon put to use
They filled it with flowers and veg and bright blooms
Until all the guy ropes came loose.

'By Gum,' said Granny, 'would you credit that
I'm surprised that nobody knew
You've heard all the rumours concerning my bloomers
They're baggy, they're big and they're blue.'

Once more the village lived up to its name
As the bloomers whirled high in the sky
When the wind stopped, the underwear dropped
On a troop of cub scouts passing by.
'Dib dib,' said Akela. 'Dob dob,' said Brown Owl.
'A gift from above sent by chance
We've left our sleeping bags back at the church
So we'll soon find a use for these pants.'

'By thump,' said Granny, 'I just don't believe it
Now the Scouts are using them too
Good job I cleaned them now they're in between them
They're baggy, they're big and they're blue.'

Later that night they all fell asleep
After eating beans, sausage and egg
You could hear all the snores drift over the moors
Twenty-six scouts down each leg
A sudden explosion shattered the night
And everyone woke with a jump
'Was it the beans or was it the wind?'
'Same thing' said one little chump.

'That's that,' said Granny, 'I just give up
I'll have to buy some that are new
For better or worse, these bloomers are cursed
They're baggy, they're big and they're blue.'

Fifty-two scouts left shivering cold
Once more the bloomers took flight
The lads looked aghast as they flew right past
And far away into the night
Like an eclipse the whole sky went dark
The moon and the stars hid from view
Voluminous bloomers sailing like schooners
They're baggy, they're big and they're blue.

Flapping away like some giant bat
Lost forever in time
The legend unfurled all over the world
From the ridiculous to the sublime
Sightings were here, sightings were there
And everyone knew they were true
Those bloomers were spotted north, south, east and west
They're baggy, they're big and they're blue.

'It's underwear, Jim, but not as we know it,
Blocking our passage ahead
Is it a timewarp or a black hole?
No it's a blue one instead.
Spock's found the rear, I've got the front here
It's final, we'll have to go through
Warp factor five, and we will survive,
They're baggy, they're big and they're blue.

Their presence was felt in our world and others
As they travelled through time and through space
Their mystical shadow dropped over Bermuda
That triangle? Gone without trace
What they did to the crew of the *Marie Celeste*
Not even Sherlock Holmes knew
There's even a photo of them in Loch Ness
They're baggy, they're big and they're blue.

Even now on those long lonely nights
In Trumpton-cum-Windy on t'moor
The story lives on in ballad and song
About those fantastical drawers.
You may think it's a myth and may not believe
But we'll tell you that everything's true
It's not empty rumours about Granny's bloomers
They're baggy, they're big and they're blue.

They're frilly, they're silly it's true
They're baggy, they're big and they're blue.

They're coming for me and for you
They're baggy, they're big and they're blue.

Look out whatever you do
They're baggy
  they're big
      and they're BLUE!

Things To Find In A Teacher's Trouser Turn-Ups

Just find any male member of staff
who wears trousers that have turn-ups
and you will usually find
that they have been wearing exactly the same pair
of trousers with turn-ups for years.
And years. And years. And years.

Imagine what can be found in those prehistoric turn-ups . . .

Crumbs from ancient sandwiches
Congealed curry stains
Two tons of belly button fluff
Dried yoghurt blobs
Dead woodlice and beetles
Flakes of mouldy chocolate
Cigarette ash
Dinosaur bones
Rusty paper clips
Bogeys
Earwax that looks like yellow cheese
Yellow cheese that looks like earwax

Whatever you do,
if you decide to have a look for yourself
be very very careful indeed
because if they see you peering at their trousers
they'll suddenly get very embarrassed
go very very red indeed,
walk quietly to the corner of the room,
turn their backs to the class
and check to see if their flies are undone.

Let's face it . . .
you wouldn't want to embarrass your teachers
in public now, would you?

Ghost Story

A very spooky story . . . join in the italics. Make up your own sound effects. Some are harder than others.

Once upon a time
Long long ago
In a far off land
Lost in the midsts of time
There was a castle
A very haunted castle
Indeed.

In the distance an owl hooted . . .
The wind was whistling . . .
A dog barked . . .
There was a tap at the door
And a sink at the window
The great oak door slowly creaked open . . .
Footsteps could be heard in the upstairs corridor . . .

Outside the storm began to rage . . . *Oooo I really am cross*
Lightning flashed . . . that'll do you thank you
Thunder crashed
There was the sound of wind breaking
all the castle's windows.
There was the sound of bagpipes playing through the
      mist . . .
As 600 headless horsemen galloped past . . .
The wind gave a low moan . . . *Oooh I'm sick of this*

Meanwhile back in the castle
The knights in armour were clanking their chains
All except for one
He was flushing his . . .

The ghosts were howling
There were ghouls howling
He was caught by the ghosties
He was caught by the g . . . surprise.
Outside the wind was still moaning . . . *oooh I'm sick of this*
The thunder still crashed . . .
The lightning still flashed . . .

Meanwhile, back in the castle
Again
Werewolves shrieked . . .
A ghostly train rattled past . . .

A ten ton anvil fell from a top turret
And landed on the cat

A ghostly voice said **Beware!**
A ghostly voice said **Beware out there**

Another ghostly voice said
**BEWARE OUT THERE THERE'S SOMETHING BIG
AND NASTY AND IT'S COMING TO GET YOU NOW**

Just then the poets heard a round of applause
And the sound of large amounts of money landing at their
  feet.

Outside the wind was still moaning . . . *oooh I can't stand this.*

Back inside the castle
The evil laughter of their tormentor rang out . . .
Who is this crazed madman?
Who could live in this castle of doom?
Who could it be?
Who could it be?

Only one person
Only one person
Only one person could live here

You can hear his footsteps creaking
You can hear his footsteps creaking

It's Mister Moore, Mister Moore
Creaking down the corridor.
Uh uh eh eh uh
Uh uh eh eh uh

Ten Things Infants Do Really Well (In Assembly When You're Reading Your Poems)

1. Not listen.

2. Not listen whilst facing different directions.

3. Girls: Not listen but pull all their little dresses over their heads at once so all you can see are miles and miles of My Little Pony knickers.

4. Boys: Not listen as they stick one thumb in their mouth and the other down their trousers. After five minutes they swap thumbs.

5. Boys: Not listen as they stick their hands down other people's trousers.

6. Not listen whilst they tell you very loudly that they have got a dinosaur on their shoe . . . look.

7. Not listen as they noisily velcro all their shoes together.

8. Not listen as they hide inside their giant pencil case.

9. Not listen as they put their hands up your trouser legs, often wearing a glove puppet.

10. Not listen as they search for the biggest bogey in the world . . . usually up someone else's nose.

You Are The Teacher –
Can You Rule This School?

1. For the first time in his life, Cecil the class softy is ever so slightly cheeky. Do you:

   a. Pretend you didn't hear.
   b. Say 'I completely understand how you feel, Cess baby, but I'd rather you didn't voice your feelings in quite so public a forum.'
   c. Give him a detention and make him cry.

2. As usual, Tracy doesn't hand in her homework and says the dog chewed it up. Do you:

   a. Believe every word and let her off.
   b. Ask if the dog's all right.
   c. Give her and the dog a detention and make them cry.

3. On Open Night a parent politely asks if 'the mark you gave my daughter wasn't a little on the low side?' Do you:

   a. Upgrade the mark immediately.
   b. See her point of view exactly without committing yourself.
   c. Downgrade the child's mark and then give them a detention for spragging on you, thus making them cry.

4. You are on yard duty and see Big Baz bashing Little Lawrence. Do you:

   a. Hide.
   b. Say 'Hey guys, enough. Let's do some Drama to shake out those negative vibes.'
   c. Join in and then give them both detention, making them cry.

5. A dinner lady offers you double chips and then double jam roly-poly pudding in front of all your pupils. Do you:

   a. Say 'No thank you.'
   b. Say 'Only if the pupils receive the same.'
   c. Scoff the lot then guzzle loads more off the pupils' plates, making them cry.

6. You are teaching Maths and realize you can't do fractions. Do you:

   a. Own up and apologize
   b. Say 'Hey, let's work this thing out together.'
   c. Drop the fractions and dish out a really tough spelling test which all the pupils fail, thus making them cry.

7. In your assembly, a pupil makes a rude noise very loudly. Do you:

   a. Ignore it, so all the school joins in to make louder ones.
   b. Check it wasn't one of the teachers.
   c. Give the whole school detention, the teachers too. They all cry.

8. You discover one of your pupils tying up a supply teacher in a stock cupboard. Do you:

   a. Run away before they tie you up.
   b. Try to see this situation from both points of view, as they're tying you up.
   c. Leave the supply teacher in there to teach him a lesson and make him cry.

9. In the staffroom a student is sitting in your seat, drinking your coffee from your mug. Do you:

   a. Say 'How nice.'
   b. Shake their hand and do some bonding.
   c. Shout a lot, demand your coffee and seat back immediately and make the student cry.

If you answered mainly:

a. You should work in Mothercare.
b. You drive a 2CV, have a Greenpeace sticker, at least one earring and wear tartan Doc Martens.
c. You are on par with Dracula, Captain Hook and Cruella De Ville. You can rule the school (but only when the dinner ladies aren't there).

**Hilarious rhymes By Paul Cookson,
David Harmer, Brian Moses and Roger Stevens**

Bestselling poets Paul, David, Brian and Roger are all ex-teachers and the perfect people to reveal what goes on inside the staffroom. You'll find out what makes your teachers tick and what they get up to at the weekend. After all, there is a lot more to your mild-mannered maths teacher than meets the eye . . .

It's a Definite Sign

Our dinner lady Mrs Mack
Is well in love with Mr Fipps
Because at every dinner time
She winks and smiles when he's in line
And gives him extra chips.

Paul Cookson

A selected list of titles available from Macmillan Children's Books

The prices shown below are correct at the time of going to press. However, Macmillan Publishers reserves the right to show new retail prices on covers, which may differ from those previously advertised.

How to Embarrass Teachers Poems chosen by Paul Cookson	978-0-330-44276-3	£3.99
Give Us a Goal! Football poems by Paul Cookson	978-0-330-43654-0	£3.99
Pants on Fire Poems by Paul Cookson	978-0-330-41798-3	£3.99
Pirate Poems By David Harmer	978-0-330-45181-9	£3.99
The Truth About Teachers Poems by Paul Cookson, David Harmer, Brian Moses and Roger Stevens	978-0-330-44723-2	£4.99

All Pan Macmillan titles can be ordered from our website, www.panmacmillan.com, or from your local bookshop and are also available by post from:

Bookpost, PO Box 29, Douglas, Isle of Man IM99 1BQ

Credit cards accepted. For details:
Telephone: 01624 677237
Fax: 01624 670923
Email: bookshop@enterprise.net
www.bookpost.co.uk

Free postage and packing in the United Kingdom